Big Machines

Big Machines Drive!

Catherine Veitch

Heinemann
LIBRARY
Chicago, Illinois

© 2015 Heinemann Library
an imprint of Capstone Global Library, LLC
Chicago, Illinois

Edited by Helen Cox Cannons and Kathryn Clay
Designed by Richard Parker and Peggie Carley
Picture research by Mica Brancic and Tracy Cummins
Production by Helen McCreath
Originated by Capstone Global Library Ltd
Printed and bound in China by Leo Paper Group

18 17 16 15 14
10 9 8 7 6 5 4 3 2 1

Cataloging-in-publication information is on file
with the Library of Congress.
ISBN 978-1-4846-0585-1 (Hardcover)
ISBN 978-1-4846-0592-9 (eBook PDF)

Photo Credits

Alamy: ©dpa picture alliance archive, 19, ©Natrow Images,
14, 15, 22c; Corbis: Demotix/© Stephen Barnes, 12, 13; Getty
Images: E+/BanksPhotos, 8, 9, front cover, VOLKER HARTMANN/AFP,
18; Liebherr: 16, 17, 22d; NASA: 4, 5, 22b, back cover; Newscom:
EPA/BERND WEISSBROD, 20; Rex Features: David Bagnall, 10, 11;
Shutterstock: justasc, 21; SuperStock: Tips Images, 6, 7, 22a, back cover

Contents

Some words are shown in bold, **like this.** You can find out what they mean by looking in the glossary.

Crawler Transporters

A crawler transporter carries rockets to the launch pad. The crawler lowers its sides and rolls under a rocket to lift it.

With its heavy load, the crawler travels only 1 mile (1.6 kilometers) per hour.

Road Trains

The longest trucks in the world are called road trains. Instead of pulling just one **trailer**, these giant trucks pull three or more.

Super
Big **Mighty**
Size

MACK

ROAD TRAIN

Road trains are found on long stretches of empty road in Canada, Australia, and the United States.

Giant Tractors

These are not your average tractors. Giant tractors have eight tires with thick grooves. The tractors weigh 10 times more than a car.

cab

Farmers climb a ladder to get into this **cab**.

Big **Super** **Mighty**
Size

groove

Combine Harvesters

Farmers use combine harvesters to separate seeds from the rest of the plant.

The Lexion 590R is one of the world's largest combine harvesters. Every minute the combine **harvests** 80 **bushels** of corn.

Monster Trucks

Adding huge tires turn these vehicles into monster trucks. Drivers show off for big crowds during competitions.

Strong bars inside the driver's cab protect the driver if the truck rolls over.

Super Truck

Meet one of the largest trucks in the world. The Terex Titan can carry two buses at once!

This truck is no longer on the road. It is now a **tourist** attraction in Canada.

Mobile Cranes

The Liebherr Company built the world's strongest and tallest crane. It can be driven to where it's needed.

boom

A long **boom** reaches high into the air.

Big **Super** Size **Mighty**

Motorcycles

The Gunbus 410 is one of the largest motorcycles in the world. It is 11 feet (3.4 meters) long.

Dream Big is a record-breaking bike. It took Greg Dunham three years to build this mega motorcycle.

GUNBUS
410

Sizing Things Up

Dream Big Motorcycle

Engine................	500 horsepower
Height...............	11.3 feet (3.4 meters)
Weight..............	2.9 tons (2.6 metric tons)
Tires	74 inches (188 centimeters)

Grave Digger Monster Truck

Engine................	up to 1,700 horsepower
Weight	5 tons (4.5 metric tons)
Tires	66 inches (168 centimeters)

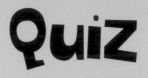

Quiz

How much of a Machine Mega-Brain are you?
Can you match each machine name to its correct photo?

crawler transporter • Terex Titan
mobile crane • road train

1

2

3

4

Check the answers on the opposite page to see if you got all four correct.

22

Glossary

boom a mechanical arm

bushel a unit of measurement used to measure amounts of corn

cab an area for a driver to sit in a large truck or machine

groove a long, narrow channel cut into a surface

harvest to gather crops, such as corn or wheat

tourist a person who travels and visits places for fun or adventure

trailer the part of a semitruck where goods are loaded and carried

Find Out More

Books

Graham, Ian. *Dump Trucks and Other Big Machines*. Mighty Machines. Irvine, Calif.: QEB Pub., 2008.

Tieck, Sarah. *Choppers*. Amazing Vehicles. Edina, Minn.: ABDO, 2011.

Websites

www.bigfoot4x4.com/history.html
www.capstonekids.com/explore/Mighty-Machines/index.html

Index